HOLY INFANCY SCHOOL

My Best Friends and Me

Emilie Barnes

WITH ANNE CHRISTIAN BUCHANAN

Illustrations by Michal Sparks

HARVEST HOUSE PUBLISHERS
Eugene, Oregon 97402

My Best Friends and Me

Copyright © 1999 Emilie Barnes and Anne Christian Buchanan
Published by Harvest House Publishers
Eugene, Oregon 97402

Mr. Gifford Bowne
Indigo Gate
1 Pegasus Drive
Colts Neck, NJ 07722
(732) 577-9333

Design and Production: Garborg Design Works, Minneapolis, Minnesota

Library of Congress Cataloging-in-Publication Data
Barnes, Emilie
      My best friends and me / Emilie Barnes with Anne Christian Buchanan; illustrations by Michal Sparks.
          p.   cm.
      Summary: Ten-year-old Emilie Marie and her friends discuss the nature of friendship. how to make a friend, and how to keep a friendship and make it special. Includes crafts, recipes, games, and other activities that friends can do together.
      ISBN 0-7369-0121-3
      1. Friendship Juvenile literature. 2. Girls—conduct of life Juvenile literature. [1. Friendship.] I. Buchanan, Anne Christian. II. Sparks, Michal, ill. III. Title.
BJ1533.F8B176   1999
177'.62—dc21
                           99-17715
                           CIP

99 98 00 01 02 03 04 05 06 07 08 / IP / 10 9 8 7 6 5 4 3 2 1

Contents

My Best Friends and Me...and You

Hi, I'm Emilie Marie, and I want to introduce you to my special group of friends. Actually, you might have already met them. We're all in a club we call the Angels.

First, there's my friend Christine. I've known her almost since we were babies. Christine is very creative and artistic, and she likes romantic stuff like princesses and flowers. The thing I like best about her is that she's an encouraging friend. She knows how to say nice things to other people.

Maria lives next door to Christine. There's always something fun and interesting going on at Maria's house, and it usually smells good because her father is a baker. I also like Maria's sweet smile and her sensible attitude. She can always figure out the simplest, best way to do something.

Aleesha is another good friend. She's very good at sports (especially soccer) and has a funny sense of humor. It's a good thing, too, because her little sister Marti is always bugging her. Aleesha loves to sing and play games, but what she likes best of all is to act in plays. She says she wants to be an actress or a singer when she grows up.

Elizabeth is sort of a new friend because her family just moved here about a year ago. Elizabeth is a real bookworm! She also loves horses and has pictures of horses all over her room. Sometimes she can be a little disorganized, but she's very smart and always willing to help somebody else if they need it. That's what I like best about Elizabeth.

Jasmine is another friend who is new. Her family just moved here, so we are just getting to know her. We've already learned that she's good at crafts, that she likes animals (especially her cockatoo, Bing), and that she's been taking violin lessons since she was really little.

I was glad to hear that, because I've just started taking cello lessons. Maybe we can play a duet together sometime! I hope so, because doing things together is something my friends and I really like to do.

Just what do we do when we're together?

The same things that you like to do with your friends. We play games. We like to pretend. We tell each other secrets. We go on walks and have adventures. We talk a *lot!*

And the last few weeks, we've been talking a lot about being friends.

Jasmine started it. She was telling us about how much she missed her friends at her old school. And then we started talking about how she can make new friends here. And before we knew it we'd thought up all kinds of ideas for making friends and keeping friends and being friends and having fun together with friends.

This was great! We wanted to learn more. So we asked other friends for ideas and talked to our parents

and looked in books, and we collected even more ideas for things to make (like gifts and crafts)…and things to do (like games and activities)…and fun ideas to make friendships even more friendly.

So that's what this book is about—being friends and doing things with friends.

It's for you and your friends— from my best friends and me.

"I'm Glad We're Friends!"

WHY FRIENDSHIPS ARE GOOD TO HAVE

Everybody wants friends. Everybody needs friends. But have you ever stopped to wonder why?

You need friends to play games with. Some kinds of fun just aren't as much fun alone!

You need friends to talk to. Friends listen to your secrets and talk with you about your problems and all the good things that happen, too. Sometimes you just need to talk for the fun of it!

You also need friends to learn from. My friends have shown me how to do all sorts of things—like roller-skate and make silhouette portraits. You need friends to give you ideas and to help you see things right. If I'm really confused about a problem, talking to a friend usually helps me sort it all out.

Sometimes you need friends to help you do things. Once Elizabeth's room got so messy she didn't even know where to start cleaning it. But the Angels all came over to help, and we had that room clean in a couple of hours!

When you have good times, you need friends to help you enjoy them. When bad things happen, you need friends even more. Friends can help you feel a little happier when you're sad and a little braver when you're afraid. You need friends to make fun things more fun and un-fun things a little easier. And you need friends so you won't be lonely.

What Is a Friend?

But what is a friend, anyway?

A friend is a person who really cares about you—the *inside* you, not just your clothes or your stuff or your other friends.

Top Ten Friends

What makes a friend a friend? Bonnie McMurren's fourth grade class at Stony Mountain School in Manitoba, Canada, took a survey to find out. They asked 198 different people from all over the U.S. and Canada, and here are the top ten answers they received. (What qualities would *you* pick?)

1. Friends can trust each other.
2. Friends help each other.
3. Friends do things together.
4. Friends are loyal to each other.
5. Friends are honest with each other.
6. Friends are people you can talk to and who listen to you.
7. Friends share with each other.
8. Friends are there in the good times and the bad times.
9. Friends never judge you. They accept you for who you are.
10. Friends have fun together.

A friend is someone who will tell you the truth...but she's also someone who cares about your feelings and tries to understand you.

A friend is someone who likes the things that you like, at least part of the time. She's somebody you enjoy being with.

And a friend is someone you can trust. She won't break promises or tell your secrets. A friend shows respect for you. She doesn't try to get you in trouble.

My Grammie always says you should choose your friends carefully. I think that means that you should make sure that everyone you call your friend really *is* your friend!

It doesn't mean that someone has to be perfect to be your friend. Nobody's perfect. But if someone wants to be your friend, she should act like a friend.

And of course, that goes for you, too.

Furry, Finny, and Feathery

Can an animal be your friend? My friends and I think so. My kitten, Angel, is a great listener, and I never feel lonely when she's purring in my lap.

Christine's dog, Micky, is a good friend to all of us, and we also like Maria's hamsters, Aleesha's fish, Elizabeth's bunny, and Jasmine's cockatoo. All my friends think of their pets as their friends—but of course we like having people friends, too!

Alike and Different

Friends don't always have to be just like you.

They can be older or younger. They can even be relatives. My Aunt Evelyn is my friend, even though she's my mother's sister. When I go over to her house, we can talk about *anything!*

Boys can be friends, too. Chad, who lives next door to Aleesha, has been her friend for a long time. They like to play basketball in Chad's driveway. And sometimes Chad and Aleesha just sit outside on the steps and talk.

Friends can come in any color, and they can be from almost anywhere. Jasmine, our new friend, was born in China and then adopted by her mom in the United States.

Maria's grandparents came from Mexico. Aleesha's family is African-American, and my mom's family is Jewish.

Elizabeth moved here from Texas, and Christine has always lived right here in this very town, in the same house where she lives now.

My friends are all a little different from each other. We like being different. Friends who are different from you can teach you interesting things.

Different friends help you think of things you hadn't thought of before. They can help you be more understanding…and that can make the whole world a better place.

But just because we're different, that doesn't mean we're *completely* different. It would be hard to be friends if we didn't have anything in common.

Here are some of the ways the Angels are alike: We're all girls. We're all about the same age. We go to the same school and don't live too far away from each other. We all like playing games and making things.

Best of all, we all care about each other and have fun when we're together. And that's the very best way for friends to be alike!

Something to Do

The "Know Your Friends" Show

Here's a fun way to find out just how well you know your friends! All you have to do is copy the questions below onto little slips of paper. (You can make up more questions if you want to.) Then fold each question in half and place in a wide-mouthed jar or a hat. Then you're ready to play.

You need at least three people for this "game show"—a "host" and at least two "contestants." The host draws a question and reads it out loud. The contestants write down their answers. Then each contestant tries to guess what the *other* person's answer was. Every right guess earns a point. After ten questions, add up the points and see who knows each other better. Now try another set of contestants, or let the host try. The person with the most points wins.

What is your favorite color?

If you could have any kind of pet, what would it be?

If you could be any animal you like, what would you be?

Name a food you really hate.

What's your favorite singer or music group? What's your favorite song?

Name a TV show you can't stand! What's your favorite TV show?

What's your least favorite chore to do at home?

What's your favorite flavor of ice cream?

If you could travel anywhere in the world today, where would you go first?

What's your favorite board game?

What's your favorite sport to watch or play?

If you could have your favorite birthday dinner, what would the main dish be?

In what state or country were you born?

Who is your favorite teacher?

If you could choose your own name, what would it be?

Name your favorite TV or movie star.

What's the best book you ever read?

How many people live at your house?

How many animals live at your house?

What is your favorite subject in school? What is your least favorite subject?

SOMETHING TO MAKE

A Picture of a Friend

This special kind of picture is called a silhouette, and people have enjoyed making them for centuries. These little pictures make super gifts for moms and dads and grandparents as well as for friends. They're really easy and fun, but it takes at least two to make one—just like a special friendship! You will need:

*a bright light, like a big flashlight or a lamp with
     the shade off
a sheet of black (or dark) paper
same-sized sheet of white (or light) paper
tape
pencil
scissors
glue stick
optional: large sheet of poster board, ruler*

1. Place the flashlight or lamp on a table a few feet from a wall. Have the subject (the person whose silhouette is being made) sit on a chair between the light and the wall so that you can see her sideways shadow

(profile) on the wall. Tape the dark paper to the wall so that the shadow falls on it. If the shadow is unclear or too big for the paper, move the light or the subject around until it's just right. If the wall is bumpy, tape a piece of poster board under the paper.

2. Ask the subject to hold very still while you trace the shadow of her head and neck on the paper. When you get to the bottom of the neck, draw a curvy diagonal line that looks like a collar.

3. Take the paper down from the wall and carefully cut out the silhouette. Center it on the sheet of lighter-colored paper and use the glue stick to fasten down all the outside edges.

4. If you wish, you can use the piece of poster board (or other paper) to make a frame. Using a ruler to make your lines straight, cut two pieces of poster board a little larger than your background paper and cut a window in one of the pieces that's big enough to frame the silhouette. Tape or glue your silhouette between the two pieces of poster board so that the silhouette shows in the window.

"Hi, I'm Emilie Marie!"
THE START OF A FUN FRIENDSHIP

Have you ever met somebody and you just knew you were going to be good friends?

That's how it was with Jasmine and me. We just looked at each other and smiled and we knew we were going to like each other.

Making new friends like that is fun. It's nice to meet someone new and get to know them and find out you have lots in common. It's nice to look forward to having fun together.

But making new friends isn't always that easy.

Sometimes you feel shy. Sometimes you don't know what to say. Sometimes you don't even know if you're going to like each other.

And sometimes, if you're new like Jasmine was this year or Elizabeth was last year, you may wonder if you'll ever have any new friends. (Of course, that's why it's important to be friendly and helpful to someone who's new.) You may even feel like everybody else already knows each other and has all the friends they need.

But guess what?

There's really no such thing as having all the friends you need. And future friends are all around you—whether you're new at your school or your town or whether you've been there all your life.

Conversation Starters

So how do you make friends when you're feeling kind of shy?

The most important thing to do is to remember to smile and look interested in the other person.

That sounds obvious, right? But if you're feeling nervous and wondering if people might not like you, it's easy to forget. You might frown or look busy or act like you don't care—and people might believe you. So it helps to think about your face and pull up the corners of your mouth. It really makes a difference.

The second obvious—but not so easy—thing to do is to say hello. If somebody doesn't do it, you both might just stand there and not say anything! So it might as well be you. Take a deep breath. Tell yourself that the other person is probably just as nervous as you are. Then put on your smile, and just say

A Friend in Any Language

Did you know that the Japanese word for friend is *tomadachi?* The Swahili word is *rafiki.* A German friend is a *Freund* (or *Freundin* if she's a girl). And girls in Spain like to have fun with their *amigas.* But in any language, a friend is still a friend!

"hi." Chances are, the other person will say "hi" back. After that, you can say anything you want. Try something like: "Hi, my name's Emilie Marie!" or "It sure is cold (or warm) in here" or "The school lunches here are better than they were at my old school."

One of the very best ways to start a conversation is with a compliment. People always like to hear nice things about themselves. So if you like somebody's sweater or her French braid or the way she's covered her math book—say so. Then maybe she'll say "Thank you," and you can keep on talking.

Asking questions is another good way to start talking to somebody. You can ask when the bell will ring or where you should go for ice cream or frozen yogurt. Or you can ask a friendly question about the other person: "Have you always gone to this school?" or "Do you have any brothers and sisters?"

Jasmine had a great idea when she first moved here. She asked the teacher's permission, then she brought pizza for the whole class! After that, everyone knew who Jasmine was!

What do you do after you get a conversation started? One good way to move closer toward friendship is to ask the other person to do something with you.

There are lots of ways to do this. Why not ask for help with a school project—or offer to help the other person with her project?

Even better, invite your future friend to sit with you and your other friends at lunch. Or ask if she can come over to your house in the afternoon or go on an outing with your family.

As you eat and talk or play miniature golf or enjoy a movie together, you'll get to know each other better, and you'll probably get to be friends, too.

The thing to remember about making new friends is to keep a lookout for friendship possibilities.

Just keep your eyes open and your smile warmed up.

What to Do When You're New

Jasmine and Elizabeth just finished being "new kids" at our school, so they put in these ideas about how a new kid can go about making friends:

1. *Be patient!* It takes time to feel like you belong—but it will happen.

2. *Keep in touch with your old friends.* When you feel alone, it's nice to remember that some people already know you and like you. So write and call as often as you can.

3. *Try to join some sort of special-interest group.* Being part of a sports team, a crafts class, a drama group, or Girl Scouts is a great way to meet people who like the same things you do.

4. *Volunteer for special projects.* Perhaps you could paint backdrops or clean up after a party. Working together with others is a good way to make friends.

5. *Get to know other new people.* You already have something in common!

6. *Remember what it's like.* When another new kid shows up, don't forget what it feels like! Say hello, introduce her to your friends, and invite her to do things with you. Then you'll have another new friend.

Something to Do

A Welcome Basket

This is a fun way to welcome someone to your town or school and start making friends with her. Find a large basket (an old Easter basket will do fine) and line it with a piece of pretty cloth. Then fill the basket with fun things to help the new kid feel welcome and at home. Here are some ideas:

· decorated pencils, erasers, etc.
· list of fun places to go in town
· snacks—trail mix, cookies, sugarless gum, etc.
· information about sports clubs, craft classes, etc.
· commercial coupons for local ice cream shops, pizza, etc.
· homemade coupons for things to do with you and your family—like go skating, come over for dinner, help wash your dog, and so on
· stamps or note paper for writing friends back home
· tiny rubber stamps and an ink pad
· an easy-to-grow plant
· a stuffed animal with a big bow
· something special from your part of the country—a sun pillow from Arizona, a sheriff's star from Texas, wild rice from Minnesota, a country music CD from Nashville, a hat or pennant from the local college or professional team

SOMETHING TO MAKE

Beaded "Hi" Pins

These little beaded pins are fun and easy to make. Wear one as a way to say "hello" to new friends or pin it on your notebook. Even better, get together with your friends to make a whole bunch of pins as gifts for teachers, parents, or anyone who could use a smile. You will need:

14 #0 (7/8") safety pins—silver or brass
1 #3 (2") safety pin—silver or brass
clear acrylic spray sealer—if you're using brass
    safety pins
a package of "seed beads" in assorted colors
1 pair needle-nosed pliers (ask your mom or dad if
    you already have one at your house)
a metal fingernail file or a dull letter opener

1. First, if you are using brass pins, spray them with the sealer to keep them from tarnishing. Ask an adult to help you do this outside. Spread the pins on newspaper, spray, let dry, turn over, then spray again.

2. Spread a bunch of seed beads out on a flat surface and look at them closely. They don't look the same! Some are thick, like little barrels, and some are flatter, like little doughnuts. The doughnut kind works best for this pin.

3. To start the pin, carefully open one of the #0 (smallest) safety pins. You're going to be stringing the beads onto the point of the pin. Now look at the chart on the next page; it shows you how to string the beads. Each square stands for one bead, and each up-and-down column of squares stands for the beads on one safety pin. For instance, column 1 is a

stack of black squares. So take that first safety pin and put seven black beads on it. Close the safety pin. (If you have trouble fitting all the beads on the pin or closing it, take all the beads off and look for flatter "doughnuts.")

4. With the pliers, carefully pinch the pin as shown to keep it from popping open. Then lay it down on the table and make another just like it—as the second column of the chart shows. Lay it down next to the first pin.

5. Column 3 on the chart is a little different. It shows one black bead, five yellow beads, then another black one. Open a third pin and put black and yellow beads on it to match the chart. (The bottom bead on the chart goes on the pin first.) Close the pin, pinch with pliers, and put it down. Repeat the process for every row in the chart. Lay the pins down on the table in the order that you finish them: 1, 2, 3, 4, and so on.

6. When you've finished putting beads on all the pins, open the big (#3) safety pin and use the nail file to push open the little loop-the-loop at the end of it. Ask an adult to help you do this. The idea is to push the loop open sideways so you can

slide the little safety pins around it. (They get a roller-coaster ride!)

7. Hold the head of the big pin in your left hand with the sharp point facing *away* from you. Pick up the *last* safety pin you beaded (number 14). Hold its head in your right hand with the beads facing away from you and slide the loop at its base onto the pointed end of the big pin. Push it down and around the loop-the-loop, then push it up the other side of the pin and up against the head. Do the same thing for all your little pins, working from right to left (the last pin you beaded to the first). Make sure that the beads on all the pins face the same way—and don't stick yourself on the big safety pin!

8. When you're through putting on the little pins, the beads should spell out "HI." Pin the big pin to your shirt or sweater and wear it.

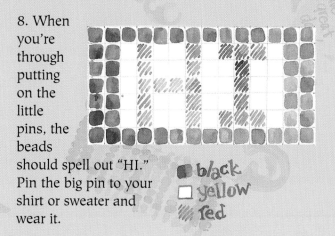

■ black
☐ yellow
▨ red

13

"We'll Always Be Together!"

TAKING CARE OF YOUR SPECIAL FRIENDSHIPS

All friends are special, but some friends are *really* special.

These are the friends you know really, really well and like a whole lot. You think alike. You understand each other. You can't imagine ever not being friends. Some people call these special friends "best friends." But I like to call my special, special friends my "forever friends."

Christine and I are like that. We've been friends a long time and can't imagine not being close to each other. We've even talked about going to the same college someday!

That doesn't mean we have to do everything together. We don't!

And it doesn't mean we can't have *other* special friends. We do! Christine's really good friends with Maria, and I've started being good friends with Jasmine.

But when I have really big news to tell, or when Christine is really sad about something, or when one of us has a fantastic idea for the Angels to do, guess who we call first? That's right. We reach for the phone and call our very special forever friend!

Finding a Forever Friend

But what if you don't have a special friend like that? Don't feel bad! Maybe you just haven't found your forever friend yet!

My Grammie says that special friends like Christine are a gift from God, and sometimes you just have to wait for them to come along. You can't *make* someone be a forever friend. You just have to wait and see.

But while you wait, there are lots of other things you can do. You can practice being a good, friendly person. And you can enjoy the friends you do have— because most forever friends start out as just ordinary, everyday friends. Then you get to know each other, and you share a lot of fun and maybe some tears, and one day you realize your friendship is really something special.

> Love is very patient and kind...If you love someone you will always believe in him, always expect the best of him... love goes on forever.
>
> THE BOOK OF
> 1 CORINTHIANS

Appreciating Your Friends

Every so often I think you should look at all your friends—especially your forever friends—and think about what you like about them and then tell them so. Every so often it's good to say, "I think you're special because…"

Sometimes it's hard to say something like that out loud. But you can say it in a card or a note. You can say it in a little tag that goes with a present you made yourself. You could put it in a song or poem and read it on an audio or video tape.

Of course, you can also say it by the way you treat your friends. When you listen to your friends, when you encourage them, when you do things their way (at least sometimes), you're really telling them, "I'm glad you're my friend."

When you remember to appreciate your friends, it makes you a better friend. And guess what? Trying to *be* a good friend is even more important than trying to *find* a good friend.

Even a forever friend!

Something to Do

The Birthday Box

This is a fun thing to do with a really special

Just Like Me!

A fun thing to do with a special friend is to have something just alike—a stuffed animal, a sweater, a little piece of jewelry. Christine and I have matching china teacups that we found in an antique store. And all the Angels have little angel-shaped candles. But you don't have to buy your look-alike treasures. How about making matching friendship bracelets or "hi" pins to remind you that you really are forever friends?

friend. It's a kind of friendship tradition that you can keep doing every year for as long as you want. And a little box is all you need to get it started!

Christine and I found a little paper-maché box at the craft store that's shaped like a heart. (It's about six inches long.) We used decoupage glue and a brush to cover it with cutouts from pretty wrapping paper. We even painted the inside of the box a beautiful pink color. And we used a gold paint pen to write "Forever Friends" on the front of the box.

The first time we used the Birthday Box was for Christine's birthday in November. I looked and looked until I found a beautiful little glass castle. I wrapped it in tissue paper and put it in the box and gave it to Christine for a gift. Now Christine had the box at her house. So when it was time for my birthday in April, Christine found an adorable little Noah's Ark tea set and tucked it in the box—then she gave the box back to me.

And that's what we do every year. We pass that box back and forth with special little gifts—a sweet little tradition from my heart to hers and back again.

SOMETHING TO MAKE

Silver-and-Gold Friendship Bracelets

"Make new friends, but keep the old. One is silver and the other gold." That's an old song my Aunt Evelyn taught me about friendship. These pretty bracelets remind me of that—they're easy to make for your new friends and your old ones—and especially for your forever friends. Look for the beads and the floss in a hobby store or large discount store. You will need:

1 package metallic silver embroidery floss
1 package metallic gold embroidery floss
13 gold 6mm beads
scissors
ruler or yardstick
craft glue
old clipboard or tabletop
tape

1. Measure and cut one piece of gold floss and one piece of silver—each 48" long—and seal the ends to keep the floss from unraveling. To do this, squeeze a little craft glue on your finger and run the end of the floss between your finger and thumb, covering the end of the floss with glue. Let the glue dry.

2. Hold the two pieces of floss together and fold them in half. You will need to have two strands (one of each color) longer than the other two. Pull one strand of silver and one of gold until they are about 30" long. Then you will have four strands of floss with a loop at one end.

Hold the floss at the loop end and carefully tie an overhand knot as shown, leaving a little loop above the knot. The loop should be just big enough for one of the beads to go through.

3. If you have a clipboard, place the knot in the "clip" part of the clipboard so that the loose ends of the thread are facing you. (If you don't have a clipboard, tape the top loop and the center strands to a table.) Arrange the threads as shown in the picture, with the short gold and silver threads together in the center and the other two longer threads on the outside. Tape the center threads down at the bottom of the clipboard. Hold their ends together and coat them with glue. Let the glue dry, then cut across the glued-together strands at an angle. This will make it easier to string the beads.

4. Now you can begin to tie the knots that make the bracelet. You will only be tying knots with the *outside* threads. The ones in the center will stay still, and you'll tie the knots around them. Each knot (a square knot) is made in two steps.
Step 1: Pick up the left-hand thread and cross it over the center and under the right-hand thread, leaving a loop on the left. Next take the right-hand thread and bring it *over* the left-hand thread, pass it *under* the center threads, and bring it up *through* the loop on the left. Pull gently on both outside threads until they form an even circle or oval around the center threads running in the middle. Then pull the circle into a *firm* knot.
Step 2: This step is just like the previous one, but backward. Pick up the right-hand thread and cross it

over the center, leaving a loop on the right. Bring the left-hand thread over the right-hand thread, *under* the center threads, and up *through* the right-hand loop. Pull the threads even, then tighten. With the two steps together, you've just completed a square knot. (Note: Working with the two colors of thread makes it easy to remember which step you just did. If you begin step 1 with the silver thread on the left, after step 1 it will be on the right. It will move back over to the left after you've finished step 2. So whenever the silver is on the left, you'll know you've finished the entire knot.)

5. Repeat steps 1 and 2 until you've completed about ½" of bracelet. Then you're ready to put on the first bead. First, untape the two center strands. Hold their ends together, take a single gold bead, and thread it onto the double center strand. Slide the bead up against the finished part of the bracelet, then tape down the center strands again.

6. Bring the two outside strands around the outside of the bead and make a square knot (two steps) right below the bead. Continue making square knots for another ½", then add another bead, then ½" of knotting, another bead, and another ½" of knotting.

7. You should now have three beads on your bracelet along with your knotting. To make a flower, slide one bead onto the center strands and three beads onto each of the outside threads. Push all the beads up against your previous work and make another square knot right below the beads, pulling the thread firmly. Adjust the beads if necessary to form the flower shape.

8. Keep on knotting and adding beads until you have three more beads. Finish with ½" of knotting.

9. To finish your bracelet, untape the center strands and hold all the strands together. Tie another overhand knot, and push it close up against the bracelet. Then tie another knot right over that one, then make another knot if necessary to make a knot just big enough to go through the loop on the other end of the bracelet. Pull all the strands in the knot really tight, then cut off the ends close to the knot. Add a little dab of craft glue at the place where you cut the ends off, just to make sure they won't unravel. Let glue dry. Fasten your bracelet by slipping the knotted end through the loop.

10. After you've learned to make this pretty bracelet, you can make it with a lot of different kinds of thread and beads. Try thick embroidery thread, natural-colored hemp, waxed-line cord, or even plain old yarn. Almost any kind of bead will work as long as the hole in the middle is big enough to go on the doubled center threads. Try making a whole bracelet out of knots and bead flowers. Or, for an interesting variation, make a bracelet using only step 1 or only step 2. The bracelet will twist around in a spiral!

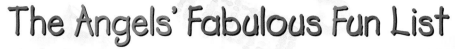

The Angels' Fabulous Fun List

FIFTY GREAT THINGS YOU CAN DO WITH YOUR FRIENDS

1. Bake cookies together and take them to a neighbor.

2. Go on a nature walk and collect interesting rocks, sticks, leaves, etc. Make a collage out of the neat things you found.

3. Collect cans or paper to recycle. Save the money you earn for a special outing together...or give it to your local food bank or children's shelter.

4. Create garbage sculptures out of old cups, pieces of paper and cardboard, bits of aluminum foil—whatever you can find. Be sure the garbage is clean before you use it!

5. Write stories and illustrate them.

6. Plant a sweet potato in a jar. Ask an adult to show you how.

7. Talk an older person into telling a story about when he or she was your age. Ask questions about how life was different or alike in those days.

8. Press flowers or leaves in a book. When dry, use to make note cards, bookmarks, and pictures.

9. Invent a pretend language or a secret code. Practice using it together.

10. Blow bubbles. Put socks on your hands and try to catch the bubbles without popping them.

11. Make and fly a kite. (See instructions on p. 22.)

12. Have everyone bring a favorite board game and spend the afternoon playing them all together.

13. Ask a parent or friend to teach a special skill—like building a birdhouse, knitting a scarf, or skipping a rock.

14. Paint look-alike T-shirts.

15. Make up your own aerobics routine.

16. Build a clubhouse or playhouse in someone's backyard using trees, bushes, plastic tarps, cardboard boxes, or whatever you can find.

17. Read a book out loud—or listen together to a book on tape.

18. Rake leaves, jump in them, rake them up again.

19. Pick up trash in your neighborhood or park.

20. Do beauty makeovers on each other—or on your moms!

21. Work on a really hard jigsaw puzzle together. Try one of those 3-D puzzles and build a bridge or a castle.

22. Draw each other's portraits with pencils or paints. Frame with cardboard.

23. Clean and decorate each other's rooms.

24. Enjoy a picnic breakfast outside—spread a blanket under a tree and have bagels, fruit, granola, or whatever. Bring milk or juice in thermoses.

25. Make paper chains and other decorations and save in a box for Christmas.

26. Borrow a video camera and make your own movie.

27. Have a backyard campout—pitch a tent or just lie out under the stars.

28. Visit a nursing home and put on a show (call to arrange this first).

29. Cook dinner for one of your families.

30. Hold a neighborhood flea market and trade toys you no longer want.

31. Have everyone bring a favorite video. Pop popcorn and watch them all together.

32. Look through albums of each other's baby pictures.

33. Write a song and sing it together. If any of you play instruments, play them along. Make it your song!

34. Set up an outdoor bowling alley using 2-liter soda bottles and a basketball. The bottles will stand up better if you put a little water or sand in each one.

35. Hold Silly Olympics for the little kids in your neighborhood. Give prizes for longest one-foot hop, best stuffed-animal head balancer, etc.

36. Go down to the high school track (if allowed) and run races.

37. Design a treasure hunt for younger brothers and sisters—be sure to make a great map!

38. Put together a bike brigade or a roller-skating rodeo—with obstacle course, races, and games.

39. Spend an afternoon creating artwork—paintings, sculpture, etc., then hold an exhibition of your works.

40. Write a group letter to a friend who has moved away. If you have an instant camera, take a picture of all of you and slip it in the envelope, too. Address the envelope and mail it before you forget!

41. Make your own gift wrap or stationary with potato prints, thumbprints, rubber stamps, or just paint.

42. Create unique clown costumes using old clothes and makeup. Each clown should have her own distinct look and personality. If you like being clowns, why not volunteer to put on a show at a day-care center?

43. Use toothpicks, felt scraps, and small fruits and vegetables to turn apples, potatoes, and other foods into cute, creative critters.

44. Find an origami book and practice making folded-paper creatures. Hang them on string from coat hangers to make mobiles.

45. Put together a newspaper for your class or your neighborhood.

46. Roll up pairs of clean socks into balls and have a sock fight. (It won't hurt!)

47. Plan a tea party and invite your moms.

48. Create your own trail mix out of cereals, nuts, dried fruits, and other goodies. Be sure to write down the recipe!

49. Learn to do some yo-yo tricks.

50. _____(your idea!)

"What Do You Want to Do Now?"

Having Fun Together

"What do you want to do now?"

Have you ever said that when you and your friends were together?

Maybe you've all come over to your friend's house, and you're sitting in her room, and you've got a whole Saturday afternoon to have fun in. Or maybe you're really bored some summer afternoon. How do you think of what to do?

A lot of people I know just seem to do the same old thing—like watch TV or play video games or go outside and ride bikes or roller skate. But we Angels

decided there are so many fun things to do in the world that we don't want to spend it doing the same old thing. So we sat down and made a long list of big and little things we can do, and whenever we get together we try to do at least one new thing on our list. We haven't even begun to do them all—and we keep thinking of stuff to add.

What kinds of different things can you do with your best friends? That depends on what you like—but here are some of the things we've done.

Grow Something

My grandfather has a big garden, and the Angels love to help him with it. This year, Papa Bob even helped us start our own Friends Garden in Maria's backyard! We each chose something to grow in it: tomatoes for Maria, pink impatiens for Christine, corn for Aleesha, sugar peas for Jasmine, and pansies for me, plus a big pumpkin patch back by the fence for Elizabeth.

I guess it was a funny little garden with all those different plants in it. But we had a great time taking care of it—even weeding was fun when we all did it together. Best of all, we got to pick tomatoes and corn and peas and beautiful flowers…and enough plump orange pumpkins to decorate all

Something to Celebrate

Did you know that the first Sunday of August is Friendship Day in the United States? Doesn't that sound like a good reason for a party?

our porches and make six yummy pumpkin pies!

Move Your Body

When you feel a little bit bored or grumpy, there's nothing like moving your body to help you feel great. And the Angels love to get moving together!

Sometimes we do exercises or move to an aerobics video. Outside, we jump rope and ride bikes and zoom up and down on our skates. We love to kick around a soccer ball or shoot baskets, even though Aleesha is a lot better than the rest of us. (We're getting better, though!) Sometimes we go hiking or to the park, and one Saturday we all made kites and went to a big field to fly them. You really have to run a lot to get a kite soaring!

Put on a Show

Aleesha wants to be an actress when she grows up, so she's always interested in putting on shows. We all like to do that, too. Sometimes we just make up pretend shows—like we're on television or something. And sometimes we even make up a whole play to present to our families. Once we did it with puppets we made. Another time we wrote a script and made costumes and everything. The audience clapped, so I guess they liked it. I know we did.

Throw a Party

The Angels really love to throw parties for ourselves and our friends and families. If you know me, you know that tea parties are my very favorite. I love to think of a theme, plan and decorate and cook, and then get all dressed up to have a nice time with my friends. But we like other kinds of parties, too—like slumber parties (sleepovers), picnics and cookouts, and of course birthday parties. We even like to help with other people's parties! And if we're kind of bored and can't think of anything to do, sometimes we'll make up a party just for us—right that minute.

Learn Something New

Who wants to learn stuff on a Saturday? We do—sometimes. There's so much neat stuff out in the world to learn about, especially stuff you don't learn about in school.

One of the most fun Saturdays the Angels ever had was the one we spent at the Children's Science Museum. We learned about how rocks are made and what air is made of and how the people of early Egypt lived. Another fun thing we did was go to a Nature Center. And the library is always a great place for fun and learning. We like to go to special programs there as well as to check out books.

And here's another way we learn to do things—from our parents and older friends. Elizabeth's mom can crochet. Maria's dad is a great baker. Jasmine's mom teaches art, and Christine's mom is a decorator. Aleesha's dad knows all sorts of things about the outdoors. Papa Bob is a gardening genius, and my mom and my Grammie know all sorts of hints for making chores easier and more fun.

So do you know what we did? We asked all these people to give us lessons. Now we can all make crocheted headbands, pumpkin pies, origami swans, and cloth-covered bulletin boards. We can pull weeds and find the constellations and even mop the kitchen floor in just a few minutes. We found out that even doing chores is easier when you learn how from an expert and then do it with a friend!

Help Somebody

Did you know that doing something for someone else can be fun? It's true! Helping others gives you a really good feeling inside—and the person you're helping feels good, too. So my best friends and I like to find things to do that make life better for someone else. So far, we've raked leaves for Mrs. Simpson down the street, taken care of our little brothers and sisters while our parents went Christmas shopping (Grammie helped), and collected toys for the local "Toys for Kids" drive. You know what we're going to do next? Learn some old-timey songs and sing them at a nursing home.

Just Be Together

Finally, you don't always have to be doing something to have fun!

Some of the best times my best friends and I have together are when we're just hanging out—sitting on Christine's big front porch or perched in Aleesha's tree house or leaning back on the big, comfy cushions in my Grammie's den. We talk. We watch TV or read books. Sometimes we plan what we are going to do next. Sometimes we just do nothing.

Do you know what?

When you're with your best friends, even doing nothing can be a whole lot of fun.

SOMETHING TO MAKE

A High-Flying Friendship Kite

This kind of kite is easy to make and fun to fly. Get together a group of friends and paint each other's faces on your kites. Then take them all to an open field on a windy day and see whose face soars the highest. To make a friendship kite you will need:

> a large sheet of wrapping paper or newsprint (36"x24") for the pattern
> 1 plastic garbage bag, "kitchen" size or larger (white ones are easier to decorate)
> 1 3/16" wooden dowel, 36" long
> yardstick and ruler
> pencil
> black permanent marker (thin point)
> scissors
> acrylic craft paints and brushes
> clear tape
> hole punch
> strips of fabric for tail
> kite string
> optional: craft knife and adult help

1. To make the pattern, use a yardstick to mark off 6" squares on the sheet of paper. (Measure off 6" sections at the top, 6" sections at the side, and connect the marks you made.) Cut it out.

2. Spread out the plastic bag on a

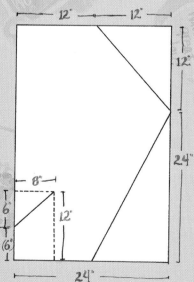

table. (If needed, cut the top and bottom so the bag lies flat.) You should have a double layer of plastic with folds on both sides. Lay the pattern with the long edge against one of the folds and trace around

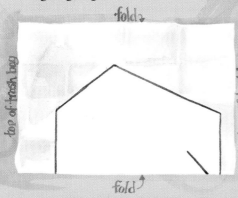

the pattern with the permanent marker. Cut out your half-kite. Cut the triangle shaped vent as shown in the diagram.

3. Unfold your kite and strengthen all the corners with pieces of transparent tape. Then decorate your kite any way you want to with acrylic paints. Since you're making kites with your friends, why not paint portraits of each other?

4. Measure 18" down from the end of the dowel and mark it with a pencil line. This is where you want to cut your dowel in half. The easiest way is to hold it down on a table with the pencil mark at the edge, then quickly break off the part that hangs off the table. This leaves sort of a ragged edge, but it won't hurt your kite. If you want a smoother cut, ask an adult to do it with a craft knife.

5. Tape the two dowel halves to the kite as shown. Use a hole punch to make holes in the outside corners. Then tape two or more strips of cloth along the bottom of the kite to make the tails. (Start with two tails about 18" long. You might need to experiment with the length and placement of the tails to help your kite fly better.)

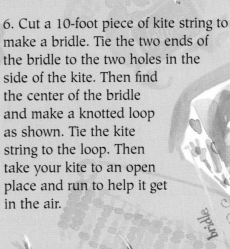

6. Cut a 10-foot piece of kite string to make a bridle. Tie the two ends of the bridle to the two holes in the side of the kite. Then find the center of the bridle and make a knotted loop as shown. Tie the kite string to the loop. Then take your kite to an open place and run to help it get in the air.

"Did Not! Did Too!"

HOW TO KEEP YOUR FRIENDSHIPS FRIENDLY

My best friends and I might be Angels…but we're not perfect!

Sometimes we have arguments and misunderstandings. Sometimes we say hurtful things to each other. Sometimes one of us will get jealous, or feel left out, or somebody will talk behind somebody else's back.

And when that happens, our friendships suddenly don't feel all that friendly!

The very worst time was last year, when Aleesha and Christine got in a big fight about something Aleesha said that hurt Christine's feelings. Then I got pulled into it, and then Elizabeth and Maria tried to help, and then we were all choosing sides and…well, it was just awful!

We didn't want that to happen again. So after Aleesha and Christine made up and we were all friends again, we decided we wanted to figure out how to avoid fights and misunderstandings and keep our friendships friendly.

Do you know the Ten Commandments in the Bible? They're a set of rules to show people how to

Ten Friendship Commandments

1. DO keep promises and secrets. Friends should be able to trust each other.
2. DON'T boss others around or tell them what to do (unless they ask!).
3. DON'T play tug of war with your friends. Everybody can have more than one friend. And acting jealous and possessive is a definite friendship buster!
4. DON'T gossip or talk behind people's backs. That always causes trouble!
5. DO try to work your problems out. If you're hurt or mad, don't just blow up in anger or sit in a corner and sulk. Go to the other person and see if you can talk.
6. DON'T tease people or put them down. That really hurts.
7. DO try to keep your sense of humor! When you can see the funny side of a problem, sometimes it stops being so much of a problem.
8. DON'T brag or show off. It annoys people, and it makes you look worse, not better.
9. DO think about others' feelings and try to understand why they act the way they do.
10. DO learn to say "I'm sorry" and "I forgive you" and "let's be friends again."

It is hard to stop a quarrel once it starts, so don't let it begin.
—*The Book of Proverbs*

have a better life.

Well, we talked a lot together and came up with Ten Friendship Commandments that can help you avoid trouble and have more fun. We liked them so much we all made a copy and put them on our walls. And they've really helped us get along better.

This Friendship Can Be Fixed!

What happens when you forget to keep the Ten Friendship Commandments? Usually you have a fight, or you get your feelings hurt, and you probably don't feel much like friends anymore. Instead, you feel angry and sad and lonely. And your friend probably feels the same way.

But this friendship can be fixed! Sometimes friendships are even better and stronger after you've learned to work through problems. But how can you do it? Basically, you follow Friendship Commandments 5 and 10! Here's how they work.

First, if you've had a fight, it's good to take some time to cool off. When you're not as mad anymore, you can start thinking about being friends again.

Next, try and think a little bit about what really happened. Was there a misunderstanding or a mistake? Were you a little in the wrong? (Probably you *both* were!) While you're thinking, try to remember why you like the other person. Think about why you'd like to be friends again.

And then...tell your friend how you feel.

But that's not easy! After a misunderstanding, it feels like there's a big wall between you. Maybe your friend is still mad.

Maybe you don't think you did anything wrong. But take a deep breath, open your mouth, and say something!

"I'm sorry" is really the best thing to say. Most of the time, you really can find *something* you're sorry about. Maybe you can say, "I'm sorry I lost my temper" or "I'm sorry I walked away and wouldn't talk to you."

If saying something to your friend's face is just too hard for you, you can send her a note or a card or a present to break the ice. The pop-up card on p. 26 is great for this. So is a bouquet of flowers. You could even send a jigsaw puzzle with a note on it: "We can work this out."

Getting Back Together

Once you've broken the ice, you need to get together to talk…and listen! You want to tell your side, but your friend wants to tell her side, too. And both of you need to understand the other person better.

When Aleesha and Christine started talking again after their big fight, they actually used a kitchen timer to make sure both of them had a chance to talk and both of them really listened. First, Christine talked for five minutes. Then Aleesha talked for five minutes. Then they did it again. Each one tried to explain how she felt and tried to understand the other person's point of view. Then they talked about how they could avoid having the same problem again. (That's where our Ten Friendship Commandments got started.)

When they were through, Christine and Aleesha called a meeting of all the Angels and apologized for dragging us into their fight. And we all apologized and told each other how much we cared about each other and how we all wanted to be friends again. You know what we did then?

Well, first we all hugged one other. Then, I went searching for some milk and leftover cookies. And Aleesha ran home and got some birthday hats and streamers left over from her sister's birthday. Then we had our own little party.

Don't you think that's a good thing to celebrate— the fantastic fact that we were all friendly friends again?

SOMETHING TO MAKE

"This Is Me" Card

This cute pop-up card is a nice way to say "Let's be friends again" after a disagreement. Once you learn how it works, you can use the same idea to make valentines and other cards, too. You will need:

1 sheet (8 ½" x 11") construction paper, card stock, or other heavy paper
1 scrap (at least 3" x 6") bright yellow construction paper, card stock, or other heavy paper
ruler
pencil
scissors
markers to decorate, including thick-line black marker
craft glue

1. Fold the 8 ½" x 11" sheet of construction paper in half and then in half again. Unfold the card and lay it down on the table in front of you like an open book, with the "inside" facing up and one of the long sides toward you. There should be two opened-up folds criss-crossing the paper, dividing the card into four equal parts.

2. Use your ruler to measure 2¼" in from the top right corner. Make a small mark there with your pencil.

Make another mark 3¼" from the corner. Make two more marks 2¼" and 3¼" from the bottom right corner. Connect the marks as shown by drawing two very light pencil lines running down the middle of the right-hand side of the card. Notice that the longer opened-out fold cuts the two lines you drew in half. Measure 1" up from this fold on each line and make another very light pencil mark.

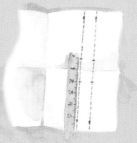

fold

3. Fold the card along the long fold you just measured from, with the pencil marks on the outside. Cut along the lines you drew from the fold to the 1" pencil marks. Now fold back the little tab you just cut out as shown, making a crease between the two 1" pencil marks. Fold the tab back the other way and crease again.

4. Unfold the card, then fold again with the short sides together and the pencil lines on the inside. Place the card before you with the fold to the left. Slip your finger under your scissor cuts and pull the cut-out piece gently toward you. The cutout will fold in the middle to form a little half-box. This is the "pop up" part of the

card. Press the card closed to crease edges of pop-up box. Then open the card and carefully erase all the pencil marks.

5. Use the bottom of a jar or bottle to trace two circles (about 2" across) on another piece of paper. Use a black marker to draw happy features on one and sad features on the either. Also, outline the faces with a thick, wavy black line to help them stand out from the card.

6. Hold the cutout card as shown in the picture and glue the bottom of the happy face to the front of the "box." Let the glue dry. Then close the card and glue the sad face on the front. Use marker to write in the message on the outside and inside of the card (see page 25). If you want to draw "sunbeams" around your happy face, do it with the card partly open so the beams are around the "popped up" face.

7. You can make all sorts of different cards using this idea. For instance, you can glue a heart instead of a happy face to the pop-up box and ask your friend to "Have a Heart." Or you can use this idea to make a birthday card or a valentine. Use your imagination.

This is me with you! Can we be friends again? Love, Annie.

"That's What Friends Are For!"

SHARING AND CARING WITH FRIENDS

We were all riding in Maria's van one day when we heard a great song on the "oldies" station. Pretty soon we were all singing along with the chorus: "That's What Friends Are Fooooooor…"

And do you know *what* that song said friends are for?

Friends are there to help each other! I really think that's true, don't you?

When you're sick or sad or lonely or scared—or just when you've had a bad day—you want your friends to be there.

And when your friends are having problems, you want to help them, too. It feels good to help other people.

The trouble is, it's not always easy to figure out *how* you can help! Sometimes you're not sure what you should do or say.

One day my friend Danielle was absent from school because her grandfather died. When she came back, she looked sad, and I felt sorry for her. I felt a little shy, too, because I didn't know the right thing to say. Finally, I just said I was sorry.

Later, I talked to the Angels about that, and they knew exactly what I meant. So we went to my Grammie, who's really good at knowing the right thing to do. (That's what *grammies* are for, right?)

Grammie said that even lots of grownups feel funny and awkward when other people have problems. She also gave us some ideas for things we can say or do if somebody we know is having problems—and also some things not to do. And after she started us thinking, we thought up some ideas of our own.

Some Helping Hints

One of the best things you can do is to look for practical ways to help. If your friend has the flu and has to miss school, you can offer to bring home her books and assignments. If she is having trouble with math, you can show her flash cards. If she's in trouble because her room is really messy and she's sad and discouraged about it, you could go over and help clean it up!

Another thing you can do when a friend is down is to encourage her. That means you think of ways to show her that you know she's having problems and you really care and you want to help if you can.

Sending a nice card is a good way to encourage a friend. So is writing a note. Or you can just talk to her and say you're sorry she's having problems. It doesn't have to be long or fancy. It just needs to say "I care."

Another nice thing to do to encourage a friend is to give her a present. It can be big, like a balloon bouquet. It can be little, like a tiny glass horse. It can be pretty, like a pansy plant in a little pot. Or it can be funny, like a silly sock doll or book of cartoons. An encouraging gift can be anything that says, "When you look at me, you know you're not alone!"

Do you know what the best gift is you can give to a friend who's having problems? A listening ear. Listening to your friend can help her figure out her feelings, and it also shows her how much you care. So if you think your friend is having a hard time, you can always say, "Do you want to talk?" Here's another

How to Know When a Friend Needs a Friend

· When she's had a bad day
· When she's sick
· When she misses someone she loves
· When a pet or family member gets sick or dies
· When there's trouble at home
· When she makes a bad grade at school
· When she's worried about something
· When she's scared
· When somebody hurts her feelings
· When she made a mistake
· Anytime *you* would need a friend if the same thing happened to you

way you can really help a friend: You can pray for her! You can talk to God about her problems and ask God to help her. I believe that really makes a difference, even if things don't work out just exactly the way I think they ought to. And I've always found that when I pray for my friends, I want to help them even more.

Finally, if a friend is going through a hard time, you can help her by being patient. Sometimes your friend might talk a lot. Or she might not be able to spend as much time with you. Or maybe she'll be thinking about her problems all the time and not be as much fun. You might even get a little tired of being a helping, caring friend.

But don't give up! Being a caring friend is really worth it—because it makes your friend feel better, because it makes you feel good, and because you might need someone to do the same thing for you someday.

And because…well, that really is what friends are for.

29

A Helping Hands Party

Here's a helping project that's fun to do *with* your friends—not just *for* them—and it can really help you be a friend to someone in need.

All you need to do is have a party. Decide on a theme, make invitations, and invite everyone in your class. Then plan and decorate and get ready for one of the most fun parties anyone ever had. In the summer, it could be a swimming party and a barbecue. In the fall, it could be a harvest celebration or a Christmas bash. It's just like any other party, except for two things…

One, it should be the liveliest, most fun party of the year.

And two, everybody is supposed to bring something. It's like bringing presents to a birthday party except you've told them what to bring…and the presents aren't for you! They're for somebody in your community who really could use a friend and a helping hand.

You could have a "Can-Do" party, for instance, and ask everyone to bring cans of food for the local food bank. Or you could have a "Let It Snow" party and have everyone bring coats and hats and gloves for the homeless shelter. Toys and books and clothes could go to a children's home.

Just be sure you tell everybody on the invitation what you plan to do with the stuff they bring. You might be surprised at how much there is. When you give them a chance, most people really like to be helping friends!

Giggle Games

These silly activities are fantastic for slumber parties or almost anytime you want a laugh:

Giggle Belly: Everybody lies on their backs in a circle with each person's head on the next person's stomach. Pretty funny already, huh? But the game hasn't even started! Choose someone to begin. She says "HA!" If she says it good and loud, the head on her stomach will bounce! That person is next. She has to say "HA HA." The next person says "HA HA HA"—and continue all around the circle until somebody loses track of how many "HA HAs" she has or you're all laughing so hard you can't go on.

Helping Hands: You need a big T-shirt or sweatshirt to do this one. Two people put on the T-shirt! One puts her head through the neck hole. The other person stands behind her (under the shirt) and puts her arms through the arm holes. From the front, you see one bulky person with one person's head and another person's arms. This double person is now going to act out a story or a poem. It's easiest if you have somebody else tell the story. The people inside the shirt have to work together to make face and hand gestures such as smiling, frowning, pointing, scratching, etc. This will be even funnier if you use a table of props—like a glass of water, some food, makeup, etc. Watch what happens when the "hands" try to bring a glass to the "head"!

Marshmallow Gobble. Wear old clothes for this one. Tie a string around the middle of a big marshmallow and dip it in chocolate sauce. Hang the string from a tree branch or the ceiling. Blindfold the first person, spin her around, then have her try to catch the marshmallow in her teeth and nibble it off the string. No hands! If she succeeds in thirty seconds, she gets a prize. Then it's somebody else's turn.

Write a Poem!

Do you like to write poems? I do. Here's a kind of poem that's fun and easy to write for a special friend. Just write her name in capital letters up and down on a sheet of paper. The letters should be on top of each other, in a straight line. Then, for every letter, write a word or phrase that starts with that letter and describes your friend. When you've finished writing the poem, copy it neatly on a nice piece of paper and give it to your friend.

Here's a word poem I wrote for Christine:

Creative
Happy
Ready for fun
Independent
Sweet
Trustworthy
Ideas are everywhere!
Never mean
Emilie Marie's friend!

Now, you try! Or if you don't want to write a poem, try painting your friend's portrait or even composing a tune for her. Use your talents to say "I'm glad you're my friend."

SOMETHING TO MAKE

Ponytail Pal

This is a great present to give to a friend who's sick or feeling down—and it's fun to make, too. If you use an old sock that's lost its mate, making this doll will cost you almost nothing! (Unless you are used to cutting and sewing fabric, ask an adult to help you with the scissors and the needle.) You will need:

1 crew sock—the kind with a smooth "foot" and ribbed top. You can make your doll any size you want, but a larger adult sock might be easiest to work with.
½ cup rice
polyester fiberfill
2 rubber bands or elastic ponytail holders
short pencil or stick to support neck
scissors sharp enough to cut cloth
tacky craft glue or fabric glue
needle and thread
to decorate your doll:
  markers, fabric paint, felt or fabric scraps, beads, buttons, charms, ribon, lace scraps, fabric glue

1. Begin by pouring the rice into the toe of the sock. This will weight your doll and help it stand upright. Then stuff in fiberfill until the doll is stuffed up to the point where the ribbed top begins. Don't stuff the sock too tightly. Poke a short piece of pencil or stick down into the middle of the fiberfill so that its top comes a little below the ribbed top.

2. Wrap one rubber band or ponytail holder tightly around the base of the ribbed part of the sock. This will make the ponytail. Wrap another rubber band more loosely (once or twice around) right below the heel of the sock to make a neck. The pencil should be more or less inside the neck. Adjust the rubber band and the fiberfill until you have a shape you like.

3. With your scissors, cut the ribbed area of the sock into long strips. Use the ribbing as a guide for making the strips more or less straight and the same size.

4. To make arms, stitch through a thickness of fiberfill on the sides. You can stitch straight down or curve slightly to move the arms forward.

5. Now the fun begins! For your doll's face, draw it on with markers, paint, or sew small beads or buttons for eyes and mouth (see example). Glued-on felt pieces work well, too. You can stitch eyelashes with brown thread. Use watercolors for soft pink cheeks or hair color.

Tie a ribbon around the ponytail—or maybe make a scarf from a fabric scrap. A tiny silk or ribbon flower is cute too. Hide the neck rubber band with some beads tied onto a piece of thread or use a fabric scrap as a scarf. You can find many fun-shaped buttons (like a flower, tea cup, or heart) at a fabric store and sew them on so your doll looks like she is holding the item. If you want to dress your doll, you can make clothes from felt, fabric, or just paint them on. You might add a paper heart with the message: "Get well soon" or "Thinking of you."